Copyright © May 2024 Sandra Pierce Mathis, EdD

All rights reserved. This document is geared toward providing exact and reliable information with regard to the topic and issue covered. The publication is sold with the idea that the publisher is not required to render accounting, officially permitted, or otherwise, qualified services. If advice is necessary, legal or professional, a practiced individual in the profession should be ordered.

No part of this publication may be reproduced, duplicated, distributed, or transmitted in any form or by any means, including photocopying, recording, or other electronic or mechanical methods, without the prior written permission of the publisher, except in the case of brief quotations embodied in critical reviews and certain other noncommercial uses permitted by copyright law. Recording of this publication is strictly prohibited and any storage of this document is not allowed unless with written permission from the publisher. All rights reserved.

The information provided herein is stated to be truthful and consistent, in that any liability, in terms of inattention or otherwise, by any usage or abuse of any policies, processes, or directions contained within is the solitary and utter responsibility of the recipient reader. Under no circumstances will any legal responsibility or blame be held against the publisher for any reparation, damages, or monetary loss due to the information herein, either directly or indirectly.

Respective authors own all copyrights not held by the publisher.

Printed by Kiyanni B., Write It Out Publishing, LLC. in the United States of America.

Write It Out Publishing LLC

Virginia Beach, Virginia

Writeitoutpublishing.com

ISBN: 979-8-9893223-5-0

Book Cover Illustrator: Maurice Rogers

Editor: Renee Johnson and Tamira K. Butler-Likely, PhD

First printing, (e-book or paperback) May 28, 2024

Sandra Pierce Mathis, EdD

Virginia Beach, Virginia

Author Email spaulett55@gmail.com

Sandra Pierce Mathis, EdD

Black Teachers and Their Experiences During Massive Resistance in Virginia 1956-1973

Historical Reflections and Contemporary Implications

VIRGINIA BEACH, VA

Sandra Pierce Mathis, EdD

Black Teachers and Their Experiences During Massive Resistance in Virginia 1956-1973

Historical Reflections and Contemporary Implications

Table of Contents

Acknowledgments	9
Dedication	11
Foreword	13
Preface	15
Chapter I *A History of the Education of Blacks in Virginia*	17
Chapter II *What Was Massive Resistance in Virginia?*	21
Chapter III *My Personal Experiences with Massive Resistance in Virginia (1961–1973)*	25
Chapter IV *Personal Reflections of Black Teachers and Their Experiences During Massive Resistance in Virginia*	31
Mrs. Elnora Louise Howard Claud (Sussex County, Virginia)	29
Mr. Joseph Pettiford (Southampton County, Virginia)	33
Dr. Mary Hatwood Futrell (Alexandria, Virginia)	37
Mrs. Gladys Howard Pettiford (Southampton and Sussex Counties)	43
A Tribute to Dr. Ruby Allen *Dr. Ruby Allen (Princess Anne County, Virginia)*	47
Dr. E. B. Howerton (Charlottesville, VA)	53
Mrs. June Skinner Banks (Norfolk, Virginia)	57
Mr. George Fauntleroy (Surry County, VA)	65
Chapter V *Where Are All the African American Teachers? —Implications for 21st Century Schools and Teachers*	69
Chapter VI *Summary and Conclusions*	75
References	77
Other Publications by the Author	79

Acknowledgments

by Sandra Pierce Mathis, EdD

Many thanks are extended to the Black teachers of the Massive Resistance Movement in Virginia who were willing to share their experiences. What an inspiration you are to all of the Black teachers in America who have followed you! This book would not be possible without you.

Dedication

This book is dedicated to my friend of thirty-nine years—the late Mrs. Elnora Louise Howard Claud—a Black teacher during Massive Resistance, who passed away on March 5, 2016. I met Louise on my first day as a teacher in 1977 and she became my very first mentor teacher and wonderful friend.

Foreword

How This Book Came to Be

I have always had a great interest in the education of Black Americans and people of various cultures and ethnicities. As a result of my interest in this topic, my dissertation addressed the needs of language minority students—most commonly referred to as English Language Learners—in five school districts in the public schools of Virginia. Upon defending my dissertation, my advisor, Dr. E. Ben Howerton, encouraged me to "keep writing." Later, upon reading my second book, Dr. C. P. Penn: An Influential African American Educator (2011), Dr. Howerton further suggested that I capture the thoughts of Black teachers who experienced teaching in the public schools during the period of Massive Resistance in Virginia. He said, "There are a few people left, so you should write about their experiences before they are all gone." Hence, this book was born out of my own personal interests and professional recommendation.

Preface

by Sandra Pierce Mathis, EdD

Massive Resistance was a policy adopted in 1956 by Virginia's state government to block the desegregation of public schools mandated by the US Supreme Court in its 1954 ruling in the case of Brown v. Board of Education of Topeka, Kansas. Who was involved? The key individual who coined the term and served as a major advocate was US Senator Harry F. Byrd, Sr., who was a conservative Democrat and former governor. Senator Byrd did not like the intrusion of the federal government in state politics, and Massive Resistance also was a reflection of his racial views and fears of his power base in Southside Virginia [7].

Massive Resistance had an impact on many individuals involved in education at that time—the Virginia Legislature, school administrators, teachers, parents, students, and the Black community at large. For the purpose of this book, the focus will specifically take a look at Black teachers during that time period. These individuals played a unique role in educating the disenfranchised Black student. In many instances in Virginia at that time, Black students were denied an education because their school was closed or because there was a different standard, or no standards set, for the education of Black children during those years.

In this book, we will look at the history of the education of Blacks in Virginia from the period of Reconstruction in 1870 to Massive Resistance—1956–1973. Who educated Black children during that time? What were their roles in society? What type of training did they receive? And what implications does this time in American history have on educating Black students today? We will also hear the voices of eight individuals who will share their personal stories and reflections of what it was like as a Black teacher during that time in Virginia's history.

Chapter I

A History of the Education of Blacks in Virginia (1865 – 1954)

The challenge of educating Blacks in America began after the Civil War ended in 1865, but more specifically around 1870, during the period of American history known as The Reconstruction. It was also the first time that the Virginia Constitution mandated a system of public education. The education of Blacks was a critical issue in America at that time and remains so today [12]. However, during that era in the history of American education, very few Black Virginians received any education at all until public schools were established. Moreover, public schools in Virginia were segregated from the very beginning without much thought or debate due to a widely held assumption that separation of races would reduce conflict [1]. Many white southerners feared Blacks would "infect" the white students based on the widely held assumption that Blacks were inherently immoral, irresponsible, and did not deserve an education. Furthermore, it was felt that providing money to educate Blacks was considered by many whites as wasting tax money [8].

When Blacks began to receive a free public education, they were thrilled. Schools were separated by race, and Black families liked the idea of their children receiving an education not subject to white interference. They felt that Black children would not be taunted or teased with racial name-calling and would therefore feel more comfortable in separate educational settings [1].

Although Black families wanted their children to receive a separate education and they were happy to receive this free education, Black schools were at the mercy of white-controlled state government funding. At that time, many whites did not want Blacks to receive an education because of a fear that Blacks would challenge white supremacy and become discontented with working in the fields or in domestic service. Thus, Black schools received far less financial support, fewer books, were housed in ramshackle buildings, and had less well-paid teachers. These issues faced by Blacks during that time marked Black Virginians with a sense of inferiority and second-class citizenship status that Blacks would have to endure throughout their lives [1].

Despite a resistance to Blacks receiving an education, several noteworthy achievements occurred during that time. First, from 1880 to 1900, literacy rates rose dramatically among whites and Blacks. However, Ayers notes that "Blacks in the south paid for schools for whites—not the other way around. The more Black citizens in a county, the greater the benefits to white students" [8].

Second, despite social and economic challenges, Blacks pursued an education with much enthusiasm. In the early 1900s, a single Black teacher taught all subjects, ages, and grades. In addition, Black schools were chronically underfunded. School attendance, especially in rural areas of Virginia, was erratic, and Virginia had one of the lowest rates of attendance in the nation in the years prior to World War II [1].

Next, Black schools in Virginia during the early 1900s were seriously overcrowded, and on the average, served 37 percent more pupils in attendance than the average white school. While most Black schools at that time could be described as primitive and made of wood, by contrast, the schools for whites were made of brick, stone, or concrete. For example, in Halifax County, Virginia in the 1937-1938 school year, the total value of white school property was $561,261, contrasted to only $176,881 for the county's Black schools [1].

During this period of struggle in educating Blacks, several individuals can be credited with providing aid to improve the education of Black children. Anna Jeanes, a wealthy Philadelphia Quaker, established a fund to employ Black "supervisors" to upgrade vocational training in Black schools in the South. As a result of this funding source, in 1908, Virginia Estelle Randolph of Henrico County became the first Jeanes Supervising Industrial Teacher. This initiative followed the precepts of Booker T. Washington, which emphasized job training and home economics as the way for Blacks to progress in life.

Another individual who helped improve the education of Blacks was Julius Rosenwald, an early partner in Sears, Roebuck & Company. Rosenwald met with Booker T. Washington in May 1911 and established a fund to improve the education of southern Blacks by building schools. Prior to his death in 1932, he had built 5,357 schools known today as Rosenwald Schools. Research indicates that Rosenwald contributed $4,400,000, the state and local government contributed $18,000,000, $1,200,000 came from other foundations, and $4,700,000 from the Black community [1].

In 1916, another important milestone in the education of Blacks in Virginia occurred when Harrison High School, a public high school for Blacks, was built in Roanoke, Virginia. Very few Black public high schools were built prior to that school, and it was not welcomed with much enthusiasm by white citizens. Prior to the completion of Harrison High School, Black students seeking a secondary education had to travel to Virginia State College in Petersburg. Finally, in 1951, the one-room, segregated Riverhill School in Grayson County is an example of how one educational facility was used to serve Black students from the first through the seventh grades [1].

Chapter II

What was Massive Resistance in Virginia?

Massive Resistance was a response by leading white politicians and public men of Virginia to resist change and fight to maintain segregated schools in Virginia by closing several public schools [5] from 1956 – 1973. However, several very important events led up to this era. Prior to the actual Massive Resistance movement, The Supreme Court decided in the landmark case, *Brown vs. Board of Education of Topeka, Kansas* (1954) that separate but equal schools were inherently unequal. In 1951, Barbara Rose Johns, a student, led a student strike at Russa R. Moton High School in Farmville that became part of this landmark decision [2].

Russa R. Moton High School, built in 1939, was designed to hold 180 students but served almost 500 students who were receiving instruction in tar paper-colored shacks referred to as "chicken coops" [2]. The school board had promised a new school, but continually delayed construction, so Johns, a 17-year-old student, organized a walk-out that forever changed the lives of Black children across the nation [6]. Johns was a great student who had many experiences traveling to schools outside of Farmville as a result of her involvement in chorus and debate, so she knew that students elsewhere were receiving better opportunities. Barbara Johns encouraged her classmates to stay out of Moton High School until it was improved [6]. Hence, four hundred fifty students walked out of Moton High School on April 23, 1951, and led a protest to the Prince Edward County School Board [5].

Furthermore, as the protest intensified within the community, Johns called Oliver Hill, the NAACP civil rights attorney in Richmond. Hill took the case and argued it before the lower courts in *Dorothy Davis et al. v. County School Board of Education*. The case went to the Supreme Court as a part of the *Brown v. Board of Education* docket where it was argued by Thurgood Marshall, the primary lawyer for the NAACP. Hill and Marshall did not argue for a new school but pressed for full integration in the white-only Farmville High School. As a result, on May 7, 1954, The Supreme Court found that racially based segregation of public school children deprived minority children of equal educational opportunities. The Supreme Court further stated that, "in the field of public education, the separate but equal doctrine has no place and that separate educational facilities are inherently unequal" [5].

Although segregation of public schools was outlawed by the Supreme Court in 1954, die-hard segregationists were unwilling to tolerate any integration anywhere in the state of Virginia. Prince Edward County responded to this decision by closing all public schools from 1959 to 1964 [2]. Furthermore, after the start of the 1958-59 school year, the governor at that time, Thomas B. Stanley, ordered schools closed in Warren County, Charlottesville, and Norfolk to prevent integration [4]. Thus, the term Massive Resistance was born. Key individuals involved included US Senator Harry F. Byrd who led the Massive Resistance movement and Garland Gray, head of the Gray Commission, which was charged with finding a way to get around or circumvent the Supreme Court decision by offering tuition tax credits to parents. Gray thought that this proposal would provide a middle ground. Although Virginians approved the tuition tax credits, later that year, the Virginia legislature embraced Massive Resistance by approving a plan that would require Governor Stanley to close schools and deny state funds to any school ordered by the federal government to mix Black and white pupils [4].

Dr. Sandra Pierce Mathis

Photo by Anita Pearson Photography, Virginia Beach, VA

Chapter III

My Personal Experiences with Massive Resistance in Virginia (1961 – 1973)

I was born in Surry County, Virginia on September 22, 1955—one year prior to the start of Massive Resistance in Virginia. I attended the all-Black Lebanon Elementary School beginning in the fall of 1961, starting first grade that year at the age of five. We did not have kindergarten in those days. The schools in the county were all Black, including teachers, students, and administrators. In September 1964, I began fourth grade at Surry Elementary School which had been an all-white school. Elementary schools at that time consisted of grades 1–7. I completed my formal education in Surry by attending Luther Porter Jackson High School from grades 8–12 graduating as salutatorian of my high school class in 1973. There were no middle schools or junior high schools in the county during my years of matriculation.

My experiences with Massive Resistance then is from the lens of a Black student, not of a Black teacher—as I am today. As I forestated, the schools that I attended in Surry County as a child were all Black, including principals, teachers, and students. However, the superintendent of this all-Black system was a white male. I spent many happy days on the sliding board and swings on the playground at Lebanon Elementary. The teachers were very strict and were always about the business of learning. As a child of that era, we knew no difference regarding education. After all, not only were the schools segregated, but so were the churches, water fountains, and doors of entry at stores.

The one personal experience that stands out for me occurred in the fall of 1964 when the schools in the county were mandated to integrate. All of the Black and white third and fourth-grade students in the county were to attend the all-white Surry Elementary School. However, on the first day of school, the Black students showed up, but no white students came. We found out later that the white students were attending school in their houses of worship. Thus, I attended fourth grade that year at Surry

Elementary, but the schools did not integrate. Moreover, eight years later when I graduated from Luther Porter Jackson High School in 1973, there were only two white teachers on the faculty (one male and one female) and one white student in my class who had come to Surry from France as part of a military family. I was taught for two consecutive years by the white female teacher, receiving instruction in American History and Sociology.

During the 1960s and 1970s, Black teachers were very much an integral part of the community in which they taught. Many of the teachers lived with Black families. For example, when we attended church on Sundays, more often than not, we saw our teachers in the pews. My first-grade teacher, Miss Bernice Henderson, lived with my cousins, Janie and Pernell Watson and when Cousins Janie and Pernell came to visit my parents on Sunday evenings, Miss Henderson often came with them!

Black teachers made home visits, personally knew our relatives, and were essentially often viewed as esteemed members of our community. In my household, for example, anything the teacher and the principal said, was viewed as the "gospel truth." My parents ALWAYS sided with the teacher and the principal. My parents believed wholeheartedly that the teacher was always right. As children, we had no voice in the matter.

All of the Black teachers in Surry County were graduates of Historically Black Colleges and Universities (HBCUs) in Virginia, North Carolina, and West Virginia (Miss Henderson's home state). Most of my teachers were graduates of Virginia State College (Petersburg, VA), Norfolk State College (Norfolk, VA), Hampton Institute (Hampton, VA), St. Paul's College (Lawrenceville, VA), Elizabeth City State Teachers College (Elizabeth City, North Carolina), and Virginia Union University (Richmond, VA). Many of my teachers lived in the community in the homes of residents, as I stated earlier. However, there were others who traveled an hour or so by car from Norfolk or Petersburg to teach in the county.

The schools that I attended in Surry County had no gymnasiums, poor heating systems, no air conditioning, but large windows. We had used books and a very basic curriculum of the three R's – Reading, Writing, and Arithmetic (we didn't call it math back then). Each day was begun with "The Lord's Prayer," The Pledge to the Flag, and Bible verses. We would also end the morning devotions with a patriotic song such as "My Country Tis of Thee" or "America the Beautiful."

My teachers were truly surrogate parents—instilling pride within us and serving as role models. How can I forget my fourth-grade teacher, Miss Henderson (who also taught me in first grade), who took me on a Trailways Bus to Richmond to buy me a white dress so that I could participate in May Day? My mother, at the time, was hospitalized and there were nine children living at home with my parents. It was my very first trip to Richmond, Virginia and I was in awe! I kept that dress for years until I became an adult. Just looking at it was such a wonderful reminder of what kindness meant from the heart of a teacher.

In 1973, I graduated from Luther Porter Jackson High School with honors and as forestated, as class salutatorian. I can truly say that my teachers from first grade through high school greatly influenced me in becoming an educator. My guidance counselor, Miss Olivia Chapman, put me in her car along with two other male classmates and took us on a tour of the campus of Old Dominion University in Norfolk. Although at the time, my first choice of a school was Norfolk State College—the same school that Miss Chapman had attended—she encouraged me to stretch myself. She said to me, "I went to Norfolk State, and it was good for me, but Sandra, predominately white colleges are looking for very good Black students and I think that it would be a wonderful opportunity for you to go there." That is another true example of the powerful influence that our Black teachers had on our lives at that time, and I am so grateful for those experiences.

Mrs. Elnora Louise Howard Claud

Chapter IV

Personal Reflections of Black Teachers and Their Experiences During Massive Resistance in Virginia

Mrs. Elnora Louise Howard Claud (deceased)
Waverly, Virginia – Sussex County 1969 – 2004
35 years total teaching in Sussex County

In 1969, I had taught only one year when four Black teachers, one man and three women (I was one of the women) were sent to an all-white high school along with approximately two hundred Black students. This was the forced integration I knew. The students didn't want to be there and neither did the teachers. I was assigned general math courses which consisted of basically all-Black students. Since I had taught only one year, it was not quite a big shock to me as it was to those who had taught longer. I was assigned a homeroom on the far end of the building. I also had to share a classroom (not the homeroom) with a white teacher. I was a floating teacher. One of the white teachers always complained about the condition of the room we shared. She complained about any paper that was left on the desk or on the floor, the arrangement of the chairs, and any writing on the desk. The blackboard was expected to be erased before she arrived in the room and before I left the room. There were never any other conversations of any type. She was an older lady who had been at the school for many years.

I experienced white parents expressing in a not-so-obvious way that their child could not be adequately taught by a Black teacher. One parent told me how she could teach the same course I was teaching her daughter. She informed me of the college she had attended and what courses she had taken.

There was one white teacher who offered help with one very difficult class of white students. They didn't want to be taught by a Black teacher and they let me know it by their actions. They were totally disruptive until this teacher came in and told them that they had to have the course and they were not going to get another teacher or class. She was another teacher who had been teaching at this school for years. Most of the time, we (Blacks) were on our own and mostly isolated in an all-white school.

Lunchtime was one of the worst times for me. Since my room was on the far end of the building and I had to make sure the classroom was in perfect condition, I usually arrived in the lunchroom late. When I received my lunch and went over to the teachers' table, all of the white teachers would get up and leave. Some were finished and some were not. They didn't want to eat with a Black person at the table. I was the only Black teacher that ate on that shift. I was left to eat alone many days. It got better over time. However, I don't remember them ever having a conversation with me during that first year. It was a relief to find no room at the teacher's table, and I would then sit and eat with the Black students.

Many of my experiences during that time I chose to forget, because this was not a time I wanted to remember.

Mr. Joseph B. Pettiford

Joseph B. Pettiford, Sr.
Southampton County, VA – 1963 – 1970
Alexandria City Schools, VA – 1970 – 1998
Years of Service – 35

Southampton County Experiences of Note

During the early to mid-sixties when "FREEDOM OF CHOICE" was the buzzword in Virginia, many of my students' parents who were sharecroppers in a predominately Peanut/Cotton Southampton County were threatened with the loss of farming and housing opportunities if they even hinted that they were anticipating taking advantage of choosing to attend Southampton High School, the all-white high school.

The local Franklin, VA, newspaper carried a notice that the State Superintendent of Public Instructions was to appear at the all-white high school to explain the State's Freedom of Choice Plan. I, the only Black in the room, attended that meeting and sat on the front row directly in front of the Superintendent!!!

After the superintendent was introduced, he promptly put his notes aside and announced that instead of giving his prepared speech, he would just answer questions from the floor!!!! Needless to say, this was a very short meeting.

Courtland, VA, the county seat of Southampton, also known as Jerusalem, the site of the famous Nat Turner Trial, was a hotbed of racism. Ms. Barnes, the business teacher at the Black Southampton County Training School—later to become Riverview High School—and one of few teachers with a master's degree, was denied the right to vote at the polls because they said that she could not READ and WRITE!!!!

It was discovered in the late '60s that 20th Century Fox was discreetly contracting with white farmers to lease farm wagons and other farm implements in preparation for a movie on Nat Turner, the Fugitive Slave, starring James Earl Jones of later *Star Wars* fame. Several of us formed an organization called the Nat Turner Foundation to represent the interests of Black landowners in the county. The cave where Nat Turner hid out was on Black-owned land and no overtures had been made to this landowner. Claudie Grant was elected president and Joseph B. Pettiford was elected treasurer of the foundation. 20th Century Fox quietly pulled out.

THE VIRGINIA CONFERENCE OF SCIENCE AND MATH TEACHERS, originally formed in 1945, proved to be a valuable asset to Black Science and Math Teachers throughout Virginia during Massive Resistance and Freedom of Choice. It allowed teachers throughout the state to identify promising Black students in Math and Science starting in grade 8, to nurture and develop them through grade 12, and to provide guidance in testing (oral as well as written), and in cooperation with the state's Historically Black Colleges, provide scholarships.

In the late 1960s, as a result of the Virginia Education Association's Salary Negotiation School, Levi Galloway, President of the Southampton County Teachers Association (Blacks were Teachers Association, Whites were Educators Association), and Joe Pettiford, Vice President of the Southampton County Teachers Association, appeared before the all-white Southampton County School Board to present a salary proposal, the first of its kind in the history of the board. We showed up with our written proposal of charts, graphs, and funding sources to support our request for salary improvement in the SALARY SCHEDULE. Then, the shock of our lives!!!! One board member said to the superintendent, "Mr. Trice, they keep talking about a salary schedule, what are they talking about?"

After turning three shades of red and pink, Mr. Trice answered, "We don't have a schedule, we kind of pay what it takes to get a teacher"!!!!! Surprise, surprise. White teachers were hired based on what they wanted!!!! Black teachers were shown a salary schedule with steps and everything!!!! That is when I decided to move to Northern Virginia where my salary for the ensuing year doubled overnight.

Dr. Mary Hatwood Futrell

Dr. Mary Hatwood Futrell

When Massive Resistance was declared in Virginia in 1956, I was a junior at Dunbar High School, a segregated school for Black students in Lynchburg, VA. Although the Supreme Court handed down its decision regarding the Brown Case in 1954, nothing changed regarding education in Virginia—segregation remained the rule of law, especially in education. Our school, Dunbar High School, had a very strong reputation, academically and athletically. The school, under the leadership of Mr. C. W. Seay, made academic achievement its top priority by ensuring that the teachers who taught us were professionally prepared and certified to teach their subject area. As students, we were inspired to achieve at our maximum level. At that time, there were only three levels defining the curriculum—academic, general, and vocational.

Upon graduation from Dunbar High School in 1958, I attended Virginia State College (now Virginia State University) where I decided to major in business education. It was at VSU that we learned that the public schools in Farmville, VA had been closed as a result of the community's refusal to desegregate. We were asked to give any books that we had from our high school years to the African American children in Farmville because they did not have books or other educational materials. I remember returning home during a break from VSU and collecting all of my books and bringing them back to VSU to be part of the collection to send to students in Farmville, many of whom did not return to "school," but those who did were being educated in churches, people's homes, etc. because they could not access the school buildings.

As part of my teacher preparation, I was assigned to complete my student teaching internship at Parker-Gray High School in Alexandria, VA, during the spring of 1962; eight years after, the Brown decision was still segregated. I completed my internship under the supervision of Mrs. Flora Chase, who was the chair of the Department of Business Education.

Upon graduation in 1962 from VSU, I applied for a teaching position in Northern Virginia but was not hired due to the surplus of applicants for teaching jobs. Thus, I worked for the federal government for a year before receiving a call from Mr. Pitt, the principal at Parker-Gray High School. He asked me if I was still interested in being a teacher. I said yes. Mr. Pitt told me that there was a vacancy at Parker-Gray and encouraged me to apply for the position, which I did, and was hired by the Alexandria City Public Schools.

I taught at Parker-Gray High School (PGHS) for two years, the two years the city was undergoing school desegregation. During my tenure at PGHS, I worked alongside Mrs. Flora Chase, who was the chair of the School's Business Education Department. I remember teaching typing classes in which I had more students than I had typewriters. Once, Mrs. Chase and I attended a citywide meeting of all the Business Education teachers at one of the white high schools. Upon entering the classroom in that school, we immediately noted how well equipped it was—every desk had a typewriter and a calculator, the very latest model. There were also workbooks for all the students. The year before, Mrs. Chase and I had submitted a request for our classrooms for new typewriters and an adequate supply to accommodate all of our students, as well as a request for workbooks for our students, but we were told the district could not afford to purchase them. Thus, we had to make copies of the assignments from the workbooks, so that our students could have hands-on experiences on how to complete projects in addition to not having enough typewriters for our classes.

In 1965, I was transferred to George Washington High School (GWHS) to be a member of its Business Education Department. I later discovered that the school district did not transfer teachers across the board but transferred those in certain programs, such as business education.

At GWHS, there were those who accepted us (African American teachers) and those who did not. I remember one of the teachers in my program one day saying to me, "I assume you know how to teach," to which I responded, "Since both of us were certified by the state of Virginia, I assume both of us knew how to teach." I also recall the school district providing professional development training to help all GWHS faculty and staff learn how to work together, especially how to work with our diverse student population. Over the course of the next five years or so, we experienced several situations that resulted in the school being shut down. One occurred when an African American student was selected to be the GWHS homecoming queen and the football captain (who was white) refused to escort her onto the playing field, which was a long-standing tradition. Another riot resulted when someone painted KKK emblems on the windows of the school one weekend. Both incidents resulted in days of rioting within the school and the school being closed to try to calm things down. A third incident resulted from the assassination of Dr. Martin Luther King, Jr., which caused another incidence of rioting in the school district, including GWHS. The unrest also spilled over into the neighborhoods surrounding the school. These types of tension to oppose desegregating the schools endured for at least half a decade and finally began to ebb as we entered the 1970s.

(Author's Note: Dr. Mary Hatwood Futrell achieved the distinction of becoming the first African American president of the Virginia Education Association (VEA) in 1976. From 1983 until 1989, she served an unprecedented six years as president of the National Education Association (NEA).

Mrs. Gladys Howard Pettiford

Gladys Howard Pettiford
Counties: Southampton and Sussex
Years of Service: 36

I graduated from North Carolina College (University now), at Durham, NC in the spring of 1962 and went to work at Southampton County Training School in Courtland, VA. When I went in for an interview with the superintendent, I was surprised when he asked what I was. I asked why. He replied, "You do not sound like…" There were no other incidents for me.

I taught Biology and General Science that first year. We had students from Prince Edward County because that county had closed all schools rather than desegregate. Students would come to live with family in the county.

The next year, the school had a name change from Southampton County Training School to Riverview High School. I do not know the politics behind the change.

I could not go back to work in the fall of 1963 because I was pregnant. I went to work in the spring of 1964 as a substitute chemistry teacher.

After a second child, I went to work in Sussex County at Central High School in the spring of 1967. I taught Biology and General Science. After my first year, the superintendent came to observe my Biology class at least once a week. He often had someone else join him. I did not get the message until he asked if I would consider going to Waverly High School to teach. Waverly High School was the all-white high school in Waverly, VA. I declined the first two times (years) he asked. I was already traveling 45 miles per day. Going to Waverly would add an extra 5 miles each way each day.

The superintendent told me before school closed in the spring of 1969 that I would be assigned to Waverly High School in the fall, along with my sister, Louise Howard, in the fall of 1969.

He also invited me to work with two persons (a Biology teacher and a young man who became principal because the former principal had left) from the high school during the summer. The three of us worked well together. The Biology teacher had taught the young man who was to become principal. She treated him as if he was still her student. We planned and outlined the lessons to be taught in the fall.

In the fall of 1969–70, Louise Howard (now Claud), Kelsir Byrd, and I, along with some Black students, were transferred to the all-white Waverly High School. We successfully integrated Waverly High School.

A Tribute to Dr. Ruby L. Allen

by Sandra Pierce Mathis, EdD

Dr. Ruby L. Allen passed away on **January 14, 2024,** two months prior to the release of this book. I am so glad that I shared with her in November, 2023 that this book was finally in publication and she was elated! It was ten years ago that Dr. Allen shared her teaching experiences with me. As a result of her willingness to participate in this book project, Dr. Allen's work will live on for many generations to come and for that I am truly grateful.

Dr. Ruby L. Allen

In the fall of 1952, I began my career as the first African American music teacher in Princess Anne County, now known as Virginia Beach, Virginia. I was hired by the school system to teach public school music in the eleven historically African American communities. The job offer was the result of repeated requests by the African American citizens, the farmers, housemaids, and "work-a-day" folk who knew that the children from their communities should have the music instruction in their schools just as those of the majority.

Music was an important part of the fabric of the eleven communities in Princess Anne County. An example of this interest in music was recorded in the minutes of the Princess Anne County Training School Association, a group of African American citizens formed to raise money to build a high school for the children in the county. Every meeting of this association always opened with music. Meetings were held in the local churches and the larger elementary schools in the county. The opening programs consisted of solos, men's quartets, women's duets, trios and quartets, church choirs, volunteer choirs, selected poetry, and debates. In some of the meetings, the musical portions of the meetings were longer than the proceedings (Princess Anne County Training School Association, 1940).

Churches in the community also showed a keen interest in music with the establishment of choir unions. Every fifth Sunday in the year, community church choirs would gather at a designated church in the county. Each choir would come prepared to sing three selections. There was always a friendly rivalry among the groups hoping by the applause from the audience that they would be considered the best choir on that Sunday. Some of the choir directors were self-taught and others studied piano or voice with a private teacher.

I became aware of the interest in acquiring an elementary school music teacher when members of the Princess Anne County Training School Association approached me. They heard that I was going to major in music at Virginia State College. They urged me to hurry and return so that they could ask Frank W. Cox, superintendent of schools, for a music teacher for their children.

When I began teaching, there were eleven community schools on my circuit. The schools had one, two, or three rooms with rows of lift-top desks, a potbellied stove, and a blackboard. Classes were multi-aged groupings of lower, middle, and upper grades. Each school had a head teacher and one or two other teachers assigned to grades 1 through 7. I was expected to go to each school once a week for a half-hour lesson in each room. Much of my time was spent traveling to the schools because they were located so far apart. Travel time was hard to anticipate because the single-lane country roads were often blocked by farmers on their slow-moving tractors, or a herd of cattle crossing the road. It was important to plan for these delays on a daily basis.

Once a week, my travel to the Blackwater School required driving my car onto a motorized wooden barge that was used to cross a small canal. On rainy days, or days when there was a high tide, the road that led to the school would flood, and I had to turn around and miss that day. I carried my meals and ate as I traveled because there were no dining places that would allow African Americans to eat while traveling on the backcountry roads.

There were no record players, music books, or rhythm instruments, but one school did have an upright piano. I was given no money for supplies, nor was I visited by the music supervisor. I was left to my own devices, to do as I wished, without any requirements to meet county music standards. My personal drive to succeed was the sole motivation for bringing music to the children in each school. Armed with my pitch pipe and my Twice Fifty-five Plus Community Songs book (Hollis, 1919), I was eager to give the children the chance to experience the joy of music through singing the folk songs, spiritual songs, patriotic songs, nursery songs, partner songs, and holiday songs found in my volume. Some of the teachers would learn the songs and sing with the children daily. Others would wait until my return to sing again.

I knew that it was important for the children to understand that music time was not "breaktime." I wanted them to look forward to the music period as a time of discovery; a time to do every song and activity, whether simple or complex, to the best of their ability. I also wanted them to enjoy the experience as well. Providing for individual differences among students in schools with multiple grades in one room was difficult. Despite the challenges, we were able to share positive musical experiences and lay the foundation for a lifelong love of music.

Four years prior to accepting the job as circuit music teacher, I was a student at the segregated Princess Anne County Training School, whose name was later changed to Union-Kempsville High School (PACTS/UK). It was to this school that I later returned to teach. It was the first high school for African Americans in Princess Anne County. The small, four-room school, built in 1938, was funded largely by African American parents who wanted a high school for their children. Four additional rooms were added to the building in 1949, which included a cafeteria and lavatories. In 1953, fourteen rooms were added providing a home economics room, an auditorium, and a gymnasium. While a student at the high school from 1948 until 1952, I achieved an education that enabled me to attend an accredited college without the need to take any remedial courses to meet entrance requirements.

My fellow students and I were taught by outstanding teachers who, despite the odds that they had faced while teaching in a segregated school system, instilled in us the will to learn, and to be the best that we could be, regardless of the times in which we lived. The faculty consisted of five instructors and a principal. These teachers lived in our communities, went to our churches, visited our homes, and attended the weddings and funerals of members of the community. They brought clothes to school for needy children, bought special books that were not supplied by the school system, and purchased school supplies for students who could not afford them. The teachers did not allow us to do work in a substandard manner. We were required to go above and beyond what we thought was expected of us. There was a special love and honor we had for our teachers. The students had a special feeling for the little school that was physically inadequate in so many ways, yet emotionally, it symbolized the courage and determination of the students who studied there. Many friendships formed between the students and teachers have remained to this day. Class reunions are still being held for classes that graduated between 1939 and 1969 when segregation ended, and this historical building was closed as a high school.

From 1953 until 1956, a part of the PACTS/UK also housed elementary classes for African American children who came from the former two and three-room schoolhouses in the northern part of the county. I was assigned to teach in this building in 1953. For the first time, once a week, single-grade music classes were included in the regular school schedule. What a thrill it was for the children and their teachers to have a single classroom for a single grade. The teachers decorated their bulletin boards and placed flowers in the rooms. Each child had his or her own desk. The bookshelves were filled with books that the teachers brought from the old buildings. The school board supplied one set of music books for each grade! Music time was special because I was able to select songs and activities that were appropriate for the grade I was visiting. I worked from a cart and traveled from room to room with a set of books, my pitch pipe, and my autoharp.

By 1956, three additional music teachers, who are the participants in this study, were hired to teach in other African American elementary schools. One of the teachers taught elementary band in the morning and high school band in the afternoon. (Please note: Dr. Allen is not referring to teachers who are included in this book. She is referring to her own study conducted for research needed for her doctoral dissertation).

In the 1956–1957 school year, I taught chorus in the high school section of the building. I remained as chorus director of the three choirs that were organized during my tenure: the mixed chorus, the girls' chorus, and the concert choir. When the school closed in 1969, the choirs had enrollments of more than 100 singers. The combined groups consistently won superior ratings in district and regional music festivals.

Dr. Everett Ben Howerton

Dr. E. B. Howerton
Retired Professor, The George Washington University
Former Virginia State Superintendent of Public Instruction

I was one of the first principals (twenty-seven years of age—Elementary) in Charlottesville during the early days of the movement. I have so often thought that I should tell the stories of how a community "made it work," and what little preparation we had to proceed. We did what came naturally, and I remember when CP (Referring to Dr. C. P. Penn, former Superintendent of Schools in Surry County, VA) spoke to us at a conference and shared insights as to "sound practices."

The dignity of "African American Teachers" and the modeling they shared was an inspiration to the rest of us. My role model was a twenty-five-year veteran of segregated schools who introduced me to the African American community leaders, preachers, and parents. In all fairness, I grew up somewhat privileged, lacked an understanding of financial challenges, and had limited exposure to the African American community. This proved to be an advantage as I was quite politically liberal and was raised to be very open-minded. My father was a member of the Lynchburg school board during "Massive Resistance" and stood firmly on desegregating as fast as possible. It was not a popular position for a bank executive to take.

I probably visited over fifteen churches to share how we were doing and received great advice. Kids were the least problematic of the challenges. Many were very poor, Black and white, which was my first exposure to the tragedy of poverty. Kids in school, however, saw no difference. Black parents were the most supportive; however, I seldom was successful in meeting with them at school. I had coffee-Pepsi cloches in homes with three to five parents at a time; generally, mothers (Which was another new experience—I seldom met fathers (if they existed). We simply talked about how we were making it work. I think I had fifty such events during my first year.

What an experience!

Black teachers always stayed late, communicated frequently with mothers or grandmothers, met on weekends, drove kids home, on and on.

Mrs. June Skinner Banks

Mrs. June Skinner Banks
Fisk University, BA Degree
New York University, MA Degree

Recently, my daughter downloaded my sixteen-year-old debutante picture on my phone. As I stare at my sixteen-year-old self, on the brink of establishing my independence, I reflect on the journey that my life has taken.

It was 1952, the year I graduated from high school in Norfolk, Virginia. I had made up my mind at the age of eleven that I wanted to go to college at Fisk University in Nashville, Tennessee, after reading about the school in *Ebony Magazine*. In those days, we didn't take SATs to get into college, we took tests for each school that we considered. I took tests for the major HBCUs at that time: Howard University, Spellman College, Fisk University, and Hampton Institute. Notice that I put Hampton last. It was the college my mother graduated from and where she wanted me to attend. I was determined not to do so since it was so close to home. As an only child, I felt that I had been under my parents' coattails too long. I attended junior high and high school where my mother was a teacher and later a guidance counselor. My father drove us to school each day. *What high school student wants to be seen surrounded by their parents all the time?* I passed all the tests and was asked to apply to all the schools except for Hampton. I deliberately put the wrong answers on that test. My mother was humiliated. She was so upset with me. However, out of 1,000 students who applied to Fisk University, my scores were in the top ten. I received a scholarship. I must add that my dad, also an only child, never pressured me to go to his colleges, Johnson C. Smith and West Virginia State.

My independence reared its assertive head when it was time for me to go to college. I lived in Norfolk, Virginia. Fisk was in Nashville, Tennessee. To get there was a twelve-hour journey. I had to take a train from Norfolk to Cincinnati and from Cincinnati to Nashville. At sixteen, I refused to let my parents accompany me. I made the trip just fine except for getting sick as the train wound around the mountains. My mother's concern for me had her visiting at Thanksgiving. That was when she found out that my PE teacher had been her classmate at Hampton. She relaxed a little after that.

In my senior year, a friend from Florida asked if I had accepted a job. At that time, I had not. She begged me to help her father out. He was the principal of a high school in Jasper, Florida. I accepted. I took a plane from Norfolk to Jacksonville, Florida. From there, I took a bus to Jasper, about two hours away. When I arrived in Jasper, the principal and his wife, the home economics teacher, met me. I was to stay with them. I had told them what I would be wearing. In those days, you dressed up when you traveled, especially by plane. I remember vividly. It was a green suit, white hat, and white gloves. They laughed when I got off the bus. They asked, "Did you think we wouldn't recognize you?" I looked around and the ladies getting off the bus looked like what we city girls called "bag ladies."

The next day, they took me to the school, which was across the street from their house. Imagine my surprise when they told me that I had to teach all the English classes and the Spanish in the high school. I was further shocked when I was shown my classroom and found a potbelly stove in the middle of my room, which I was supposed to fuel each day. At twenty and being a city girl, I wasn't looking forward to this task. However, as fate would have it, I didn't have to worry about it because many of my eleventh and twelfth-grade boys were older than I was, and they delighted in making fires and bringing me gifts like sandwiches and even a live turkey. In those days, boys who lived in rural areas often didn't go to school because they worked on farms helping their families out.

I spent a year in Jasper and in 1957 took a job in my hometown of Norfolk. What a difference a change in location makes. I was assigned to Ruffner Junior High School as an English teacher. After leaving small classes of twenty or fewer students where I was held in high esteem, I faced classes of fifty or more students. In some classes, I had forty-five boys and five girls. This was the era of Massive Resistance. The students came from low-income communities and often reflected a lack of home training, indications of gang groupings, and lack of exposure to what was expected as acceptable behavior in school. We were expected to visit the homes of our students. This gave us an insight into our students' environment. I have a vivid memory of visiting the home of one of my students and seeing the mattress that he slept on in the living room covered by a sheet that looked like it had been dipped in coal dust. Another vivid memory took place on a field trip to Virginia Beach, a suburb of Norfolk at that time. I will never forget a chubby young man sitting up front on the side seat. He kept looking out of the windows. As we left the familiar surroundings of downtown Norfolk and emerged into the beautiful suburbs of Virginia Beach, this young man exclaimed, "Is there only one family living in these homes?" as he observed the beautiful brick homes in the Thoroughgood neighborhood. He had never ventured outside of his neighborhood of dilapidated houses and housing projects. Our textbooks were discarded books from the white schools. Pages were missing or torn. During my tenure at Ruffner, schools were closed during Massive Resistance. Black churches opened their doors to educate Black students.

In 1962, I married the love of my life, John L. Banks, a Master Sergeant in the US Army. He insisted that I go to summer school and get my master's degree. African American educators could go to the best schools out of state and the state would pay for their education rather than have them go to its lily-white schools. I chose to go to New York University. My mother was also enrolled. She was getting a second master's in guidance. She had received her first master's from Columbia University in child development. I majored in speech education with the expectation of becoming a speech pathologist. I graduated in 1966 and entered the Speech Pathology Department in Norfolk Public Schools. There were three African Americans in the department at the time, and we could only work with African American students with speech, hearing, and language problems.

Reliving my life's journey as I look back at my sixteen-year-old self, I recall that in 1968, life began to change for me in a myriad of positive ways. First, I became pregnant after trying for many years. My husband was sent to Germany for three years in January and I was supposed to join him at the end of the school year. I also got an opportunity to help shatter the racial barrier at Old Dominion University in Norfolk, Virginia. At the time, the only African American faculty member was A. B. Jackson, the renowned artist. I was asked by the chair of the Speech Department, Dr. Reuben Cooper, to teach public speaking as an adjunct professor. You can imagine the audible gasps that were emitted when I stepped up to the podium to begin class. However, that turned out to be an enjoyable experience for me, except when I was hospitalized frequently from complications with my pregnancy. During those times, I asked a friend, a Jewish coworker, to substitute for me. My students let me know that they preferred me teaching the class. One student asked if his father could audit the class. At the end of the semester, they presented me with a custom-made gavel set that I continue to cherish.

At the end of the school year, as fate would have it, my water broke the day after school was out and I was hospitalized for five weeks. My beautiful baby girl was born on July 16, 1968, eleven weeks early and weighing only 2 lbs. and 14 ounces. I was not allowed to hold her or touch her. She remained in the hospital for two months until she weighed 5 lbs. I was unable to travel to Germany with her until she became more stable. Therefore, I returned to my job as a speech therapist in Norfolk Public Schools. I was given an offer to return to Old Dominion University to teach a voice and diction class, in addition to my public speaking class. I declined due to having a newborn at home who still needed careful attention. Junelle was fourteen months old at the end of the next school year and we were cleared to go to Germany.

In Germany, we lived on the economy. That means we did not live in military base housing. We lived in a beautiful apartment building that housed a Ford dealer and his family in the apartment above us, a German teacher who taught English, and his wife, a ballet dancer, who lived on the third level. The fourth level was empty when Junelle and I moved in. After living there for a couple of months, an army private and his family moved in while awaiting base housing. They were a young white family and I befriended them. One day, a strange thing happened. The young wife was visiting me. I told her that I was going to take a bath. She startled me when she asked if she could accompany me because she had never seen a Black person naked and she wanted to see if they were the same color all over. Of course, I responded, "No." I did tell her I was the same color all over.

After living in Zweibrucken, Germany, for a couple of months, I became bored. My husband was managing two clubs, the Rod and Gun and the Golf Club. He wasn't home until late at night. I was used to working and couldn't find enough to do to fill the void. I decided to visit a friend who was teaching in Ramstein, which was about 40 US miles away. She informed me that her principal was looking for a reading teacher. I was certified to teach reading on a secondary level, so I made an appointment for an interview with the principal. The interview went well, and he was happy to hire me, but he asked if I knew that a high school was opening in my hometown. If I got hired there, I could avoid the commute, especially in bad weather. He would be happy to hire me if that didn't work out.

I made an appointment with the principal of the DOD high school in Zweibrucken. After meeting me, he told me almost immediately that they had no openings. A gentleman sitting in his office asked if I had ever taught college. When I told him that I had taught at Old Dominion University in Norfolk, Virginia, he let me know that he might have a place for me on the college level. The principal became interested and asked if I had a master's degree. When I told him that I had a degree from New York University, he announced that he did, too. All of a sudden, a job became available. I was hired as the Chairman of the English Department. I was often left in charge of the building when the principal had to leave.

My last chance to crack the glass ceiling of Massive Resistance came when I returned home to Virginia in 1970. Mr. Setzer, head of the Special Education Department, Norfolk Public Schools, asked me not to go back to the English Department. Although he didn't have an opening in the Speech Department, he did have an opening in the Special Education Department. I was informed that there was a wing opening at Rosemont Junior High that was just for special education students. If I took a position, I would get a position in speech pathology as soon as one became available. Of course, I didn't turn the offer down. The problem was that I had never taught special education students in a classroom setting. I called a friend in Richmond, Virginia, who worked in the State Education Department. She gave me a crash course. At that time, Educable Mentally Retarded students were not receiving academic learning. They did a lot of arts and crafts projects. I was not good at that. I ended up teaching my special needs students the way I usually taught with modification. They went to the library and they had homework. Parents of students in other classes asked that their children be taught like the students in my class. By the way, the students were white. This was the first time a Black teacher had taught a classroom of white students in the system. I continued to break barriers when a position came open in the Speech Department. I took the place of a white therapist who went out on maternity leave. Her students were white. This was the beginning of desegregation in the Speech Department.

The journey of the sixteen-year-old girl who set out on her life's adventures at a tender age continued to take her to heights of achievement in her profession and in life's pursuits.

Mr. George L. Fauntleroy

Mr. George L. Fauntleroy–Surry County, Virginia

Black Teachers and Their Experiences During Massive Resistance in Virginia: Historical Reflections and Contemporary Implications (1956-1973)

My experiences as a Black teacher began in 1970. I graduated from a segregated, all-Black high school, George P. Phenix, in 1965, in the city of Hampton. After graduating from high school, I attended Norfolk State College. I graduated with a BS degree in music education. I received my Master of Education in administration and supervision from Virginia State University in 1989.

During the summer of 1970, I received a phone call from the principal of Surry Elementary School in Surry County, inviting me to come to Surry County to be interviewed for a teaching position in music education. The public schools in Surry County during the 1960s and beginning 1970s had all Black students enrolled. The white students attended the all-white Surry Academy. The families of the white students resisted integrating in 1968 and opened the all-white Surry Academy. The all-white member school board boarded up the white schools to keep the Black students from attending the all-white Surry High School. The superintendent of the schools was white.

The population of Surry County was 65 percent Black but had an all-white school board. During the 1950s and 1960s, many Blacks were denied voter registration rights and could not vote. The white high school had a gymnasium and swimming pool. I was surprised during my tour of the Black schools that the high school did not have a gymnasium. The Black students had physical education outside or on the stage of the auditorium. The girls' and boys' basketball teams had to practice outside on a dirt basketball court. The school did not have a marching or concert band program. The school did not have a kindergarten program.

The Black students had a high drop-out rate because many of the boys had to work on county farms. Farming was the number one industry in Surry County. The school morale was at its lowest for students and teachers. Teacher salaries in Surry County in the sixties and early seventies were one of the lowest in the state of Virginia. Many teachers did not have teacher certifications.

I was drafted in the US Army from 1971 until 1974. While serving in the army, I kept in contact with a number of the citizens in Surry. There was a massive voter registration drive in 1972. Many Black citizens received voting rights for the first time and four Black citizens were elected to the five-member school board. Four Black citizens were also elected to the five-member board of supervisors. After the election of four Black school board members, major changes began in the school district. Teacher salaries improved and teachers had to be certified by the Virginia Department of Education to teach in Surry. Student state test scores started to improve.

The first Black superintendent of schools, Dr. Clarence Penn, was employed in 1976. After taking control of the Surry County Public Schools, Dr. Penn discovered that public tax funds were illegally being given to the private, all-white Surry Academy. He immediately cut off the public funding to the private Surry Academy. Surry Academy no longer could stay in business and merged with Tidewater Academy of a neighboring county. Under Dr. Penn's administration, the Surry County Public Schools state test scores continued to improve, all teachers were certified to teach in all academic areas, teacher salaries improved, and the morale of the teachers and students improved tremendously. During my teaching career, I experienced the transformation of a school district that went from rags to riches.

George L. Fauntleroy, MEd Retired Principal 1970–2007

Chapter V

Where Are All the African American Teachers? —Implications for 21st Century Schools and Teachers

(Adapted from an article by the author that was published in the Virginia Journal of Education, December 2017)

During your years of schooling from kindergarten through grade 12, have you ever been taught by a Black teacher? This question might strike you as odd, but statistics indicate that there has been a considerable decline in the number of Black teachers in American schools. Current research indicates that the racial and ethnic makeup of our teaching corps has not kept pace with the rapidly expanding diversity in our nation's public school population and for that reason, educators are concerned about the lack of role models for minority youth [14]. Furthermore, with 50 percent of low-income Black students dropping out of high school, taking a look at the teaching force in this country could provide insight into that problem [3].

The shortage of Black teachers has become of such concern that former US Secretary of Education, Arne Duncan, established the TEACH-for initiative, recruiting more Black teachers among the ranks of teachers in America. The TEACH campaign was designed to raise awareness of the teaching profession and to get a new generation of teachers, especially more males, into the classroom [3]. Likewise, John Legend, a popular singer, musician, and education activist, has established a platform for increasing the number of Black teachers in our nation's schools with the goal of ending education inequality in America's schools [3].

One other program, Call Me MISTER (Men Instructing Students Toward Effective Role Models), is the creation of the Clemson University Research Foundation and three historically Black institutions in South Carolina: Claflin University, Benedict College, and Morris College. A national initiative currently in place at colleges such as Longwood University in Farmville, Virginia (Byrd et al., 2011), Call Me MISTER is designed to increase the number of minority males in the classroom with an emphasis on the lower performing elementary schools [14]. Both Former Secretary Duncan and Mr. Legend have appealed to US college students to invest in the future by teaching [3].

What does America's teaching force really look like? According to the National Center for Education Statistics (NCES), in 2007–2008, 83 percent of public school teachers were Caucasian, while 7 percent each were Black or Hispanic, 1 percent each were Asian or of two or more races, and less than 1 percent each were Pacific Islander or American Indian/Alaska Native. Further research supports those findings indicating that with nearly 3.5 million public school teachers in the United States, only about 17 percent of the teaching workforce consists of underrepresented minorities. Black students comprise about 16 percent of our public school students, but Black teachers only represent 8 percent of the teaching workforce [11]. A more recent article by the Commonwealth Institute of Virginia stated that over 75 percent of the licensed teachers in Virginia self-report as white, 11 percent as Black, and only 3 percent as Hispanic [19].

Why is the number of Black teachers in America's schools so important, you might ask? Well, there are a number of reasons. First of all, Black students need role models and need to see themselves reflected in the professional community. Second, Black teachers have similar cultural experiences and linguistic backgrounds which allow students and teachers to have familiar interactions (10; 11). In one study on improving the academic achievement of African American students, the students stated that they were most successful in school when the teachers took a personal interest in them and when they perceived that they were being treated equally [12]. In that same study by Mathis (2010), racial issues were mentioned overwhelmingly as students' perceptions were of being treated differently by teachers as a result of their race. Next, additional Black teachers in the classrooms will inspire Black students to pursue higher education. Finally, Black teachers provide awareness to non-Black faculty and administrators regarding diversity within subgroups of the Black race and how to work with the parents of those students (10; 11).

The National Education Association (NEA) and the Center for American Progress are deeply concerned about this "diversity gap" at elementary and secondary schools across the country. These groups want more to be done so that the teaching force mirrors the students in the classrooms [10]. Moreover, as Former Secretary Duncan stated, "There are just not enough African American teachers. I'm actually working very hard traveling throughout the country to make sure our teacher workforce reflects the diversity of our students. There's a growing imbalance in terms of what our teachers and principals look like in relation to our students." [3]. With 50 percent of low-income African American students dropping out of high school, more African American teachers in the classroom could make a huge difference [3].

What are the reasons for the shortage of African American teachers? There are various reasons for this. One reason is that historically, the number of African American teachers began to decline after desegregation [11]. As a result of the Brown ruling in 1954, thousands of African American teachers lost their jobs as a result of the busing of Black students to majority-white schools to achieve racial balance in the schools. Thirty-nine thousand Black teachers in seventeen states lost their jobs from 1954 to 1966 [11]. The Black teachers who kept their jobs experienced internal re-segregation and were only allowed to teach Black students while the white teachers were allowed to teach white students at so-called integrated school sites [11].

More contemporary issues affecting the number of Black teachers include the inadequate academic preparation of basic skills while in K–12, which leaves many minorities undereducated and unable to meet the demands and rigor of higher education [11]. While serving as a university professor in teacher education at an HBCU in Virginia, this author observed that many of the Black students enrolled in the teacher education program, for example, were unable to pass the state assessments needed to become fully certified teachers. Although the university provided labs for practice, many of those same students were employed in full-time jobs and therefore had a limited amount of time to access this opportunity online or lacked transportation to come back to the campus to take advantage of this opportunity. I also found that the pre-service teachers enrolled at this university needed a great deal of mentoring on how to navigate the process and on how to prepare for these assessments. As a result of these issues, many Black education majors dropped out of the teacher education program and enrolled in other majors such as Psychology or Interdisciplinary Studies. Moreover, they could not afford to continue to pay for assessments as this process would prolong their matriculation at the university.

Another issue that has influenced the number of Black teachers in public schools includes more opportunities to choose a different career path other than education. Prior to the Brown ruling in 1954, teaching was considered a prestigious, middle-class occupation. Today, some Blacks consider teaching "as a career of the bygone era" [11]. Dr. C. P. Penn, a Black man who was a retired Superintendent of Schools in Surry County, Virginia, spoke proudly about education as a service to others [13]. As a result of more opportunities for Blacks, especially women, to enter more lucrative careers such as medicine, business, law, and architecture, there has been a significant decline of African American teachers [11].

What do Blacks have to say about this shortage? According to an article in the Austin Weekly News, Disappearing Acts: The Decline of Black Teachers, Brandon Johnson, the author, stated that Black teachers are more likely to work in high-poverty schools with high percentages of Black students having severe challenges. He further stated that these schools tend to be less desirable workplaces with a high turnover in school administrators, relentless testing, and a lack of teacher autonomy over curriculum and where the schools are more likely to be closed than "turned around" [9].

What can we do to improve or alleviate this diversity gap? First, strong academic preparation is needed, starting in kindergarten through high school, and prior to entering college and a teacher education program. Moreover, stronger secondary school preparations, specifically in reading, writing, and math are needed. The stronger the K–12 program, the better Black students will perform on state-mandated teacher assessments of basic skills. Next, organizations such as Future Teachers of America (FTA) and Future Educators of America (FEA), sponsored by Phi Delta Kappa International, are needed in more American high schools to attract the top Black students into the teaching profession. In Virginia, as recently as 2019, Norfolk State University, an HBCU, housed The Future Teachers' Academy [19]. Third, nontraditional and alternative routes to teaching could be another solution to this dilemma [11]. With this method, teachers with an earned bachelor's degree are allowed to enroll in this program through extensive coursework and a lengthy apprenticeship-type program, or by entering a classroom with only one week of formal training outside of the classroom [11]. There are various models of the nontraditional route to teaching. Finally, mentor teachers—retired or currently employed—are needed, who are willing to follow the progress of these students as they enter and matriculate through a teacher education program.

So where are all the Black teachers? Let's find them. Let's mentor them. Let's train them and make a concerted effort to place them back in our public schools. Our children and society in general need them.

Chapter VI

Summary and Conclusions

The education of Blacks has been an important issue in Virginia since the period of Reconstruction in 1870. Furthermore, Brown vs. Board of Education of Topeka, Kansas (1954) and Massive Resistance also played important roles in the education of Blacks in Virginia from 1956–1973. During that time, many Blacks did not receive an education or acquired a substandard education due to underfunding of the public schools for Black students. It is important to note, however, that although Blacks were denied a comparable education--underfunding, dilapidated buildings, and outdated books—to whites at that time, it was the Black teacher who truly made the difference in the lives of Black children and their future success.

The testimonies of the seven Black teachers, as well as Dr. Howerton's experiences as a white administrator working with Black teachers and students, all corroborate the experiences of that time period. It is important to note that several Black teachers of the Massive Resistance period were asked to share their experiences, but only seven were willing. Some of those teachers were reluctant and even today, more than fifty years later, feared they would receive a backlash for being open and revealing the experiences of Black educators and what it was really like at that time.

So, what do we know about Black teachers of the Massive Resistance era in Virginia and Black teachers of today? Are there parallels? It is very likely that in this nation, we are still feeling the effects of the loss of the Black teacher as a result of Massive Resistance and the integration of public schools. Although the Black race has thrived in education, there remain many challenges, especially the Black teacher shortage of today. Is it likely that this country never recovered from the loss of so many Black teachers who were not accepted in the white schools as a result of integration? A recent article on teacher burnout presented many of the challenges that teachers of color continue to face, including pandemic-era burnout, low pay, and growing demands placed on Black teachers across the country, especially for those who work in underfunded schools with fewer resources [10].

An article in Education Week provided some of the answers to the Black teacher shortage of today and many of the issues faced by them. First, "The State of Teacher Diversity in American Education" (2015), stated that nationally nonwhite teachers are hired at a higher proportion than other teachers, but they also leave the profession at a higher rate. Second, further research on the topic by Travis Bristol, a research and policy fellow at the Stanford Center for Opportunity Policy in Education, explored what it takes to keep the minority male teacher in the classroom [15]. He found that many nonwhite educators feel voiceless and therefore not capable of bringing about change in their schools. However, many lone Black male teachers in the study expressed staying in their schools because of favorable conditions, despite feeling "disconnected" from their school's mission. Black students who are the racial minority in schools have expressed the same feelings [15]. In Boston, for example, loner teachers felt as if they were viewed primarily as behavioral managers and second as teachers. Moreover, many felt that their colleagues considered them intellectually inferior [15].

Finally, it appears that the experiences of many Black teachers of today echo the voices of the seven Black teachers who were willing to share their experiences during this period. Despite the innovations in technology and better physical school plants and adequate funding, Black teachers are expressing a disconnectedness in the school setting. It is that crucial piece that really needs to be fixed in order to effect change. Many school divisions are trying to increase and/or keep minority teachers through growing their own through high school programs. However, wisdom dictates that school administrators read what these seven extraordinary teachers had to say about their experiences during Massive Resistance in Virginia and learn from them.

References

1. Beginnings of Black Education— The Civil Rights Movement in Virginia (An Exhibition on Display February 7 – June 19, 2004). Retrieved on 8/6/2013 at http://www.vahistorical.org/civilrights/education.htm

2. Bowers, I. (12/9/2015). Civil Rights Secret Revealed. The Virginian Pilot. Norfolk.

3. Certain, T. (2014). Secretary Duncan and John Legend call for more Black teachers in the classroom. National Congress of Black Women.

4. Diaries reveal race disputes. (September 25, 1996). Alexandria, Virginia. *Alexandria Journal*.

5. Digital Resources for U. S. History. (2013).

6. Green, K. (2015). Something must be done about Prince Edward County (A family, a Virginia town, a civil rights battle). New York. HarperCollins Publishers.

7. Hershman, J. (2011). Massive Resistance. Retrieved February 18, 2013, from Encyclopedia Virginia at http://www.EncyclopediaVirginia.org/Massive_Resistance.

8. History Engine: Tools for collaborative education and research. Retrieved on 8/6/2013 at http://historyengine.richmond.edu/episodes/view3956

9. Johnson, B. (2013). Disappearing acts: The decline of black teachers, Austin Weekly News.

10. Levy, M. (2023). Teachers face burnout, low pay, and politics (Educators of color especially feel heat, triggering an exodus). *The Virginian Pilot*, August 10, 2023.

11. Madkins, T. (2011). The Black teacher shortage: A literature review of historical and contemporary trends. The journal of negro education, Vol. 80, no. o. 3. Pp. 417 – 427.

12. Mathis, S. (2010). Improving the academic achievement of African American Students (A practical guide for principals, teachers, students, and parents). Chesapeake, Virginia. Maximilian Book Press Publishers.

13. Mathis, S. (2011). Dr. C. P. Penn: An influential African American educator. Chesapeake, VA. Maximilian Book Press Publishers.

14. Mathis, S. (2017). Where are all the African American Teachers? *Virginia Journal of Education*. Vol. 111, No. 3.

15. Mitchell, C. (2/17/2016). Black male teachers a rarity. Education Week.

16. National Center for Education Statistics (January 24, 2014). Fast Facts, Teacher Trends.

17. Nation at a Glance (May 5, 2014). U. S. teachers not as diverse as their students, The Virginian Pilot, Norfolk, Virginia.

18. Sawchuck, S. (2/17/2016). Preservice programs seek to head off teacher biases. Education Week.

19. Thecommonwealthinstitute.org (2019). Representation matters: why and how Virginia Should Diversify Its Workforce.

20. Virginia Journal of Education. (2015). Call me mister program boosts minorities in teaching, Vol. 108, No. 5, Page 27.

21. Virginia's Massive Resistance to school desegregation. Retrieved on 8/6/2013 at http://www.vcdh.virginia.edu

Other Publications by the Author

1. Improving the Academic Achievement of African American Students: A Practical Guide for Principals, Teachers, Students, and Parents (2010)

2. Dr. C. P. Penn: An Influential African American Educator (2011)

3. Why Should I Go to School? (2019)

4. Cooking with Love Just Like My Mama Taught Me (Authentic Virginia Cuisine) (2020)

5. Children's Literature by Black Authors (A Culturally Responsive Approach to Reading Instruction Pre-K Through Grade 5) (2023)